Arizona
Facts and Symbols

by Emily McAuliffe

Consultant:
Gwen Russell Harvey
Director of Education
Arizona Historical Society

Hilltop Books
an imprint of Franklin Watts
A Division of Grolier Publishing
New York   London   Hong Kong   Sydney
Danbury, Connecticut

Hilltop Books
http://publishing.grolier.com

Library of Congress Cataloging-in-Publication Data
McAuliffe, Emily.
   Arizona facts and symbols/by Emily McAuliffe.
   p.cm.—(The states and their symbols)
   Includes bibliographical references and index.
   Summary: Presents information about the state of Arizona and its nickname, motto,
and emblems.
   ISBN 0-7368-0080-8
   1. Emblems, State—Arizona—Juvenile literature. [1. Emblems, State—Arizona.
2. Arizona.] I. Title. II. Series: McAuliffe, Emily. States and their symbols.
CR203.A8M38 1999
979.1—dc21
                                                                        98-15808
                                                                            CIP
                                                                            AC

Editorial Credits
Mark Drew, editor; James Franklin, cover designer and illustrator; Sheri Gosewisch,
   photo researcher

Photo Credits
Chuck Place, 6, 16
One Mile Up Inc., 8, 10 (inset)
Photo Network/Sal Maimone, 10
Root Resources/Anthony Mercieca, 12
Unicorn Stock Photos/Bob Barrett, cover
Visuals Unlimited/Doug Sokell, 14; Beth Davidow, 18; Nathan W. Cohen, 20; Barry
   Slaven, 22 (top); Jeff Greenberg, 22 (middle); Mark E. Gibson, 22 (bottom)

Table of Contents

Nevada

Utah

Colorado

Grand Canyon

ARIZONA

New
Mexico

California

Colorado River

Phoenix

Arizona-Sonora
Desert Museum

Tucson

OK Corral

Tombstone

Mexico

○ City
✪ Capital
〜 River
🏛 Places to
Visit

Fast Facts about Arizona

Capital: Phoenix is the capital of Arizona.

Largest City: Phoenix is the largest city in Arizona. More than 1 million people live in Phoenix.

Size: Arizona covers 114,006 square miles (295,276 square kilometers).

Location: Arizona is in the southwestern United States.

Population: 4,554,966 people live in Arizona (U.S. Census Bureau, 1997 estimate).

Statehood: Arizona became the 48th state on February 14, 1912.

Natural Resources: Arizonans mine copper, coal, and silver.

Manufactured Goods: Arizonans make computer parts, building supplies, and dairy foods.

Crops: Arizona farmers grow cotton, lettuce, and other vegetables. They also raise cattle and sheep.

State Name and Nickname

No one is certain how Arizona got its name. It may have come from the Tohono O'odham (TOE-hone-oh AH-ah-tom) words al (AHL) and schon (SHOHN). Together the words mean little spring. The Tohono O'odham are a group of Native Americans.

Arizona's best known nickname is the Grand Canyon State. The Grand Canyon is in northwestern Arizona. It is a deep valley with steep sides. The Colorado River wore away rocky land to form the Grand Canyon.

The Grand Canyon is the largest canyon in the United States. It is about 217 miles (349 kilometers) long. It is 18 miles (29 kilometers) wide in places. Parts of the canyon are more than one mile (1.6 kilometers) deep.

Another nickname for Arizona is the Copper State. Each year, Arizona produces more copper than any other state.

The Grand Canyon is in northwestern Arizona. It is the largest canyon in the United States.

State Seal and Motto

Arizona adopted its state seal in 1911. The state seal is a symbol. It reminds Arizonans of their state's government. The seal also makes government papers official.

Arizona's state seal shows a miner, farm fields, and cattle. They stand for Arizona's most important businesses. The seal also has a river and a dam. They show how important water is to this dry, hot state.

Arizona also has a state motto. A motto is a word or saying that people believe in. Arizona's state motto is "Ditat Deus." It means "God enriches." To enrich means to improve something or someone. It also means to make wealthy. Arizona's founders hoped to become wealthy from the state's many natural resources.

People in the Arizona Territory adopted their motto in 1864. They kept this motto when the territory became a state.

Arizona adopted its state seal in 1911.

State Capitol and Flag

Arizona's capitol building is in Phoenix. Phoenix is the capital of Arizona. Workers built Arizona's capitol with stone found in the state. They finished the building in 1900.

Government officials once worked in Arizona's capitol. But the number of officials increased over time. The building could not hold all of Arizona's officials. Today, officials meet in buildings near the capitol to make Arizona's laws.

Arizona's capitol is now home to the Arizona State Capitol Museum. Visitors learn about Arizona's history there.

Arizona's government adopted the state flag in 1917. The top half of the flag has 13 rays. These rays stand for the original 13 colonies. The flag has a copper-colored star in the middle. The star stands for Arizona's copper mines.

Arizona's capitol building is in Phoenix.

State Bird

The cactus wren became Arizona's state bird in 1931. Many cactus wrens live in Arizona's deserts.

Cactus wrens build nests shaped like bulbs. These birds make many nests but live in only one. The false nests confuse enemies. Enemies cannot be certain which nest is a wren's home. Female wrens lay four or five eggs each year in one of their nests. The eggs are white with brown spots.

Cactus wrens often build nests on cactuses. Cactus needles help protect wrens and their young from enemies.

Adult cactus wrens grow to be about eight inches (20 centimeters) long. Their heads and necks are mostly dark brown. The wrens have a white stripe above each eye.

People can easily recognize cactus wrens by their song. Cactus wrens chug when they sing. They sound like small train engines.

Cactus wrens often build nests on cactuses.

State Tree

The paloverde (pal-oh-VUR-dee) is Arizona's state tree. Paloverde is the Spanish word for green tree. The paloverde became the state tree in 1954.

Paloverdes grow well in Arizona because of the state's climate. Much of Arizona is dry and sunny. Arizona's days can be very hot during summer.

Paloverdes are short and sturdy. They grow to be about 30 feet (nine meters) tall. Their bark is yellow-green. Paloverdes have short branches. The branches do not have leaves for most of the year. The trees have small, oval leaves during spring.

Paloverde trees produce yellow blossoms. They usually bloom in April or May.

Paloverdes grow well in Arizona's dry and sunny climate.

State Flower

The saguaro (suh-WAH-roh) cactus blossom is Arizona's state flower. It became the state flower in 1931.

Saguaro cactus blossoms have large, white petals. Petals are the colored outer parts of flowers. The blossoms bloom in the spring. May is the best month to see cactus blossoms.

Saguaro cactus blossoms grow on saguaro cactuses. These cactuses grow only in the Sonoran Desert. A large part of this desert is in southern Arizona.

Saguaros have thick branches that point upward. The branches make the cactuses look as if they have arms. Cactus blossoms bloom on the tips of saguaro branches.

Saguaro cactus blossoms have large, white petals.

State Mammal

The ringtail became Arizona's state mammal in 1986. A mammal is a warm-blooded animal with a backbone. Warm-blooded means that an animal's body heat stays about the same. Its body heat does not change with the weather.

Ringtails look like cats. Their eyes and ears are large and round. Their tails are bushy and have black and white bands. Their tails can be 12 to 17 inches (30 to 43 centimeters) long. Adult ringtails grow to be 24 to 32 inches (61 to 81 centimeters) long.

Ringtails live in dens. Their dens are usually in cliffs or other rocky places. Many ringtails make dens in the Grand Canyon.

Ringtails leave their dens at night to hunt. They eat bugs, snakes, and small mammals. They also eat fruit and berries.

Ringtails have bushy tails with black and white bands.

More State Symbols

State Reptile: The ridgenose rattlesnake became Arizona's state reptile in 1986. Ridgenose rattlesnakes are venomous. Venomous snakes have poisonous bites. Ridgenose rattlesnakes live in pine forests in southeastern Arizona.

State Amphibian: The Arizona tree frog became the state amphibian in 1986. Arizona tree frogs have sticky toes that help them climb.

State Fish: The Arizona trout became the state fish in 1986. Arizona trout live in streams throughout the state.

State Fossil: Petrified wood has been the state fossil since 1986. Petrified wood is wood that has turned to stone over time. People can see petrified wood in Arizona's Petrified Forest National Park.

State Gemstone: Turquoise became Arizona's state gemstone in 1971. Turquoise is a blue-green stone that people use to make jewelry.

Ridgenose rattlesnakes live in pine forests in southeastern Arizona.

Places to Visit

Tombstone

Tombstone is a town in southeastern Arizona. Visitors see the OK Corral there. A famous shootout took place at the OK Corral. Visitors also see Boot Hill Cemetery. Many famous gunfighters are buried there.

Arizona-Sonora Desert Museum

The Arizona-Sonora Desert Museum is in Tucson. It is an outdoor zoo and garden. Visitors see rattlesnakes, tarantulas, and scorpions in natural surroundings. They tour a prairie dog village and a bat cave. Visitors also see cactuses and other desert plants.

Grand Canyon

The Grand Canyon is in northwestern Arizona. Visitors hike around the rim of the canyon. They ride mules or hike to the canyon bottom. Visitors also camp in the canyon. Some visitors take rafting trips on the Colorado River.

Words to Know

blossom (BLOSS-uhm)—the flower on a plant or fruit tree
canyon (KAN-yuhn)—a deep valley with steep sides; a river wears away rocky land to form a canyon.
enrich (en-RICH)—to improve something or someone; enrich also means to make wealthy.
mammal (MAM-uhl)—a warm-blooded animal with a backbone
motto (MOT-oh)—a word or saying that people believe in
petals (PET-uhlz)—the colored outer parts of flowers
symbol (SIM-buhl)—an object that reminds people of something else; the U.S. flag is a symbol of the United States.

Read More

Capstone Press Geography Department. *Arizona.* One Nation. Mankato, Minn.: Capstone Press, 1996.

Cone, Patrick. *Grand Canyon.* Minneapolis: Carolrhoda Books, 1994.

Filbin, Dan. *Arizona.* Hello USA. Minneapolis: Lerner Publications, 1991.

Fradin, Dennis Brindell. *Arizona.* From Sea to Shining Sea. Chicago: Children's Press, 1993.

Useful Addresses

Arizona Office of Tourism
2702 North Third Street
Suite 4015
Phoenix, AZ 85012

Arizona Secretary of State
1700 West Washington Street
Phoenix, AZ 85007

Internet Sites

Arizona Facts
http://www.primenet.com/~randmo/azfacts.htm
50 States and Capitals
http://www.50states.com
Grand Canyon Explorer Home Page
http://www.kaibab.org

Index